STEAMPUNK Darlings™

Coloring Book
Illustrated by Hannah Lynn

CW01475063

"Trixie"

"Sadie"

"Evelyn"

"Jacqueline"

"Railroad Rendezvous"

"Harriet"

"Sonja"

"Belle of the Ball"

"Nova"

"Cascade"

"Cordelia"

"Briella"

"Rabbit in a Hat"

"Vivian"

"Melody"

"Norah"

"Kat"

"Luna"

"Quinn"

"Stella"

"Everly"

"Curiosity"

"Bridget"

"Morgan"

"Jessie"

e Elements
He
B C N O F Ne
Al Si P S Cl Ar
Ge As Se Br Kr
Sn Te I Xe
Pb Bi Po At Rn
Uut Uuq Uup Uuh Uus Uuo
Dy Ho Er Tm Yb Lu
Cf Es Fm Md No Lr

Elements

Printed in Great Britain
by Amazon